Born in 1946

By

Kerry Butters.

Born in 1946

Millennium:	2nd millennium
Centuries:	19th century – **20th century** – 21st century
Decades:	1910s 1920s 1930s – **1940s** – 1950s 1960s 1970s
Years:	1943 1944 1945 – **1946** – 1947 1948 1949

1946 (MCMXLVI) was a common year starting on Tuesday (dominical letter F) of the Gregorian calendar, the 1946th year of the Common Era (CE) and *Anno Domini* (AD) designations, the 946th year of the 2nd millennium, the 46th year of the 20th century, and the 7th year of the 1940s decade.

Contents

Events

January

- January 6 – A revised and streamlined revival of Kern and Hammerstein's *Show Boat* opens on Broadway at the Ziegfeld Theatre.
- January 7 – The Allies recognize the Austrian republic with 1937 borders, and divide the country into four occupation zones.

January 10: First meeting of UN.

January 10: Project Diana

- January 10
    - The first meeting of the United Nations is held at Methodist Central Hall Westminster in London.
    - *Project Diana* bounces radar waves off the Moon, measuring the exact distance between the Earth and the Moon, and proves that communication is possible between Earth and outer space, effectively opening the Space Age.
- January 11
    - Enver Hoxha declares the People's Republic of Albania, with himself as prime minister.
    - Porfirio Barba-Jacob's ashes go back to Colombia.
- January 16 – Charles de Gaulle resigns as a head of a French provisional government.
- January 17
    - The United Nations Security Council holds its first session at Church House, Westminster in London.
    - United States Senator Dennis Chávez (D-NM) calls for a vote on a Fair Employment Practice Committee bill which calls for an end to discrimination in the workplace. A filibuster prevents it from passing.
- January 19 – The Bell XS-1 is test flown for the first time (unpowered), with Bell's chief test pilot Jack Woolams at the controls.
- January 20 – Charles de Gaulle resigns as president of France.
- January 22
    - Iran: Qazi Muhammad declares the independent people's Republic of Mahabad at the Chahar Cheragh

Square in the Kurdish city of Mahabad. He is the new president, Haji Baba Sheikh is the prime minister.

- The National Intelligence Authority and its operational arm the Central Intelligence Group are established in the United States; these become part of the Central Intelligence Agency in 1947.

January 28: *Bluenose* founders.

- January 25 – The United Mine Workers rejoins the American Federation of Labor.
- January 28 – The Canadian schooner *Bluenose* founders on a Haitian reef.
- January 31
  - The last session of the Permanent Court of International Justice occurs.
  - Yugoslavia's new constitution, modeling the Soviet Union, establishes 6 constituent republics (Bosnia and Herzegovina, Croatia, Macedonia, Montenegro, Serbia and Slovenia).

February

- February 1
  - Trygve Lie of Norway is selected as the first United Nations Secretary-General.

- The Kingdom of Hungary becomes a republic, heavily influenced by the Soviet Union.
- February 14
  - The Bank of England is nationalized.
  - ENIAC (for "Electronic Numerical Integrator and Computer"), an early general-purpose electronic computer, is unveiled at the University of Pennsylvania.
- February 15 – Canada indicts 22 communist agents.
- February 20 – An explosion kills more than 400 coal miners in West Germany.
- February 24 – Juan Perón is elected president of Argentina.
- February 28 – In Philadelphia, General Electric strikers and police clash.

March

- March 2
  - British troops withdraw from Iran according to treaty; the Soviets do not.
  - Ho Chi Minh is elected President of North Vietnam.
- March 4 – C. G. E. Mannerheim resigns as president of Finland.
- March 5 – In his speech at Westminster College, in Fulton, Missouri, Winston Churchill talks about the *Iron Curtain*.
- March 6 – Vietnam War: Ho Chi Minh signs an agreement with France which recognizes Vietnam as an autonomous state in the Indochinese Federation and the French Union.
- March 7 – The 18th Academy Awards ceremony is held. Best Picture goes to *The Lost Weekend*.

- March 9
  - Juho Kusti Paasikivi becomes president of Finland.
  - Bolton Wanderers stadium disaster at Burnden Park, Bolton, England, 33 killed and hundreds amongst the injured
- March 10 – British troops begin withdrawing from Lebanon.
- March 15 – Clement Attlee promises independence to India as soon as they can agree on a constitution.
- March 19
  - The Soviet Union and Switzerland resume diplomatic relations.
  - French Guiana, Guadeloupe, Martinique and Réunion become overseas *départements* of France.
- March 22 – The United Kingdom grants Transjordan, as it is then known, its independence; 3 years later the country changes its name to Jordan.
- March 29 – The Gold Coast has an African majority in its parliament.

April

- April 1
  - A 14-meter high tsunami strikes Hilo and Laupāhoehoe on the Big Island of Hawaii; 173 are killed, thousands injured.
  - The Malayan Union is formed.
  - Singapore becomes a Crown colony.
- April 3 – Japanese Lt. General Masaharu Homma is executed outside Manila, the Philippines for leading the Bataan Death March.

- April 10 – In Japan, women vote for the first time, during elections for the House of Representatives of the 90th Imperial Diet.
- April 17 – Syria's independence from France is officially recognized.
- April 18
  - The inaugural session of the International Court of Justice (ICJ) occurs.
  - The United States recognizes Josip Broz Tito's government in Yugoslavia.
  - The League of Nations, in its last meeting, transfers its mission to the United Nations and disbands itself.
- April 23 – The Eastern Pennsylvania Basketball League (Which is now the CBA) is founded.
- April 27 – FA Cup: Derby County beat Charlton Athletic in the first FA Cup final since 1939.
- April 28 – Pestalozzi Children's Village (*Kinderdorf Pestalozzi*) established at Trogen in Switzerland to accommodate and educate orphans of World War II according to Pestalozzian principles.
- April 29 – Trial against war criminals begin in Tokyo; the accused include Hideki Tōjō, Shigenori Tōgō and Hiroshi Ōshima.

May

- May 1 – At least 800 Indigenous Australian pastoral workers walk off the job in Northwest Western Australia, starting one of the longest industrial strikes in Australia.

- May 2 – Six inmates unsuccessfully try to escape from Alcatraz Prison. A riot occurs, the "Battle of Alcatraz".
- May 7 – Tokyo Telecommunications Engineering (later renamed *Sony*) is founded with about 20 employees.
- May 9 – King Victor Emmanuel III of Italy abdicates, and is succeeded by his son Umberto II.
- May 10
  - Jawaharlal Nehru is elected leader of the Congress Party in India.
  - The first V-2 rocket is successfully launched at the White Sands Missile Range.
- May 20 – The British House of Commons decides to nationalize mines.
- May 21 – At the Los Alamos Laboratory, Dr. Louis Slotin saves his coworkers but receives a fatal dose of ionizing radiation (the incident is initially classified).
- May 22 – The Hashemite Kingdom of Transjordan is founded.
- May 25 – The parliament of Transjordan makes emir Abdullah their king.
- May 26 – Czechoslovak parliamentary election, with Communist victory (38%), last before communists take power.
- May 31 – A Greek referendum supports the return of the monarchy.

June

- June 1
  - Ion Antonescu, prime minister and "Conducator" (Leader) of Romania during World War II is executed; he was found guilty of betraying the Romanian people for benefits of Germany and sentenced to death by the Bucharest People's Tribunal.
  - D'Argenlieu, French High Commissioner for Indo-China recognizes an autonomous "Republic of Cochin-China" in violation of the March 6 Ho–Sainteny agreement, opening the way for conflict between the Viet Minh and France.
- June 2 – In a referendum, Italians decide to turn Italy from a monarchy into a republic. Women vote for the first time.
- June 3 – The Interpol organization re-founded, telegraphic address "Interpol" adopted.
- June 6 – The Basketball Association of America is formed in New York City.
- June 8 – In Indonesia, Sukarno incites his supporters to fight Dutch colonial occupation.
- June 9 – In Thailand, King Bhumibol Adulyadej (Rama IX) accedes the throne after the mysterious death of his brother, King Ananda Mahidol (Rama VIII).
- June 10 – Italy is declared a republic.
- June 13 – Umberto II of Italy leaves the country and goes into exile in Portugal; Alcide De Gasperi becomes head of state.
- June 14 – The Baruch Plan is proposed to the United Nations
- June 17

- o A tornado on the Detroit River kills 17.
- o Laurence Olivier's *Henry V* opens in the United States nearly 2 years after its release in England. It is the first Shakespeare film in color, and critics hail it as the finest film of a Shakespeare play ever made.
- June 23
  - o 1946 Vancouver Island earthquake.
  - o The National Democratic Front wins a landslide victory in the municipal elections in French India.
- June 25 – International Bank for Reconstruction and Development (IBRD) (World Bank) begins operations.
- June 30 – The War Relocation Authority is abolished.

July

- July 1 – Nuclear testing: Operation Crossroads, a series of nuclear weapon tests conducted by the United States at Bikini Atoll in Micronesia, is initiated by detonation of *Able* at an altitude of 520 feet (158 m).

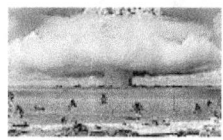

- July 25: Undersea Atomic Test Baker
- July 4
  - o Ankara University is founded in Turkey.
  - o After more than 380 years of Western dominance, the Philippines attains full independence.
- July 5 – Bikinis go on sale in Paris.
- July 7

- - Mother Frances Xavier Cabrini becomes the first American saint to be canonized.
  - Howard Hughes nearly dies in a test flight of the Hughes XF-11, which crashes in a Beverly Hills neighborhood due to a propeller malfunction.
- July 16 – Bureau of Land Management (BLM) within Department of the Interior (formed by merger of Grazing Service and General Land Office).
- July 21 – An Irgun bomb explodes in Jerusalem due to secretive talks between Jews and Britain to consolidate the state of Israel.
- July 22 – King David Hotel bombing: The Irgun bombs the King David Hotel (headquarters of the British civil and military administration) in Jerusalem, killing 90.
- July 25
  - Nuclear testing: In the first underwater test of the atomic bomb, the surplus USS *Saratoga* is sunk near Bikini Atoll in the Pacific Ocean, when the United States detonates the *Baker* device during Operation Crossroads.
  - At Club 500 in Atlantic City, New Jersey, Dean Martin and Jerry Lewis stage their first show as a comedy team.
  - In the last mass lynching in the United States, a mob of white men shoot and kill two African-American couples near Moore's Ford Bridge in Georgia.

August

- August 1
    - The United States Atomic Energy Commission is established.
    - The Fulbright Program, a system of U.S. international educational exchange scholarships, is established.
    - The Hungarian forint is introduced in Hungary by the government, ending the world's biggest hyperinflation in the country.
    - The Scandinavian Airlines System is founded as a consortium of the flag carriers of Sweden, Denmark and Norway.
- August 3 – Holiday World, originally called *Santa Claus Land*, opens to the public at Santa Claus, Indiana. It becomes the first themed park, preceding Disneyland by 9 years.
- August 4 – The 1946 Dominican Republic earthquake (magnitude 8.0) hits the northern Dominican Republic, killing 100 and leaving 20,000 homeless.
- August 16
    - Direct Action Day: Violence between Muslims and Hindus in Calcutta begins "The Week of the Long Knives" which leaves 3,000 dead.
    - The All Hyderabad Trade Union Congress is founded in Secunderabad.
    - The Kurdistan Democratic Party is founded in South Kurdistan.
- August 18 – The Vergarola explosion in Croatia kills 70.
- August 25 – American golfer Ben Hogan wins the PGA Championship.

September

- September 2 – The Interim Government of India takes charge, with Jawaharlal Nehru as Vice President, as part of the transition from the British Raj to full independence for India and Pakistan.
- September 4 – Street violence between Muslims and Hindus erupts in Bombay.
- September 8 – Bulgaria is declared a People's Republic after a referendum; King Simeon II leaves.
- September 24 – Cathay Pacific Airways is founded in Hong Kong by American Roy Farrell and Australian Sydney de Kantzow.
- September 28 – George II of Greece returns to Athens.

October

- October 1 – Mensa, an international organization for people with a high intelligence quotient (IQ), is founded by Roland Berrill, an Australian-born lawyer, and Dr Lancelot Ware, an English biochemist and lawyer, in Oxford.
- October 2 – Communists take over in Bulgaria.
- October 6 – Sweden's Prime Minister Per Albin Hansson dies in office of a heart attack.
- October 10 – Commencement of the Noakhali genocide of Hindus in Bengal at the hands of Muslim mobs.
- October 11 – After a few days of vacancy, the Swedish premiership is taken over by Tage Erlander .
- October 13 – France adopts the constitution of the Fourth Republic.

- October 14 – International Organization for Standardization (ISO) founded.
- October 15 – Nuremberg trials: Hermann Göring, founder of the Gestapo and recently convicted Nazi war criminal, poisons himself two hours before his scheduled execution.
- October 16
  - The remaining ten Nazi war criminals sentenced to death at the Nuremberg trials are executed by hanging in a gymnasium in the Nuremberg Palace of Justice.
  - The United Nations' first meeting in Long Island is held.

November

- November 1 – In the first Basketball Association of America game, the New York Knicks defeat the Toronto Huskies 68–66 at Toronto's Maple Leaf Gardens.

- Flag of UNESCO
- November 4 – UNESCO established as a specialized agency of the United Nations.
- November 5 – Senate and House elections in the United States both give majorities to the Republicans.
- November 10

- At least 1,400 people are killed in an earthquake measuring 7.4 on the Richter magnitude scale, in the Ancash Region and Quiches District in Peru.
- The Slimbridge Wetland Reserve opens in England.
- November 12
  - A truce is declared between Indonesian nationalist troops and the Dutch army in Indonesia.
  - In Chicago, a branch of the *Exchange National Bank* (now part of the LaSalle Bank) opens the first 10 drive-up teller windows.
- November 15 – The Netherlands recognizes the Republic of Indonesia.
- November 17 – Eight British servicemen are killed in Jerusalem by Jewish nationalists.
- November 19
  - Afghanistan, Iceland and Sweden join the United Nations.
  - Romanian general election, 1946: The Romanian Communist Party wins 79.86% of the vote through widespread intimidation tactics and electoral fraud.
- November 22 – Tony Benn is elected as Treasurer of the Oxford Union.
- November 23
  - Vietnamese riot in Haiphong and clash with French troops. The French cruiser *Suffren* opens fire, killing 6,000 Vietnamese.
  - The Workers' Party of South Korea is founded.
- November 27 – Cold War: Indian Prime Minister Jawaharlal Nehru appeals to the United States and the Soviet Union to end nuclear testing and to start nuclear disarmament, stating

that such an action would "save humanity from the ultimate disaster."

- November 29 – The All Indonesia Centre of Labour Organizations (SOBSI) is founded in Jakarta.

December

- December 1 – Miguel Alemán Valdés takes office as President of Mexico.
- December 2 The International Whaling Commission was signed in Washington, D.C. to "provide for the proper conservation of whale stocks and thus make possible the orderly development of the whaling industry".
- December 7 – A fire at the Winecoff Hotel in Atlanta, United States kills 119.
- December 11 – UNICEF (the United Nations Children's Emergency Fund) is founded.
- December 12
  - The United Nations severs relations with Franco's Spain and recommends that member countries sever diplomatic relations.
  - Léon Blum founds a government of socialist parties in France.
  - Iranian troops recapture the Azerbaijan province and the Kurdish Republic of Mahabad, both of which had seceded earlier in the year.
- December 14 – The International Labour Organization becomes a specialized agency of the United Nations.
- December 15 – The first election to the Representative Assembly of French India was held.

- December 16 – Siam joins the United Nations (changes name to Thailand in 1949).
- December 19 – Viet Minh forces begin a war against French occupying forces in Vietnam, succeeding in 1954 with France's surrender at the Battle of Dien Bien Phu.
- December 20
  - Frank Capra's *It's a Wonderful Life*, featuring James Stewart, Donna Reed, Lionel Barrymore, Henry Travers, and Thomas Mitchell, is released in New York.
  - At least 1,362 people are killed in an earthquake and associated tsunami in Japan.
- December 22 – The Havana Conference begins between U.S. organized crime bosses in Havana, Cuba.
- December 24 – France's Fourth Republic is founded.
- December 25 – The first artificial, self-sustaining nuclear chain reaction in Europe was initiated within the Soviet (Russian) nuclear reactor F-1.
- December 26
  - The Flamingo Hotel opens on the Las Vegas Strip.
  - David Lean's *Great Expectations*, based on the Charles Dickens novel, and featuring John Mills, Valerie Hobson, Martita Hunt, Alec Guinness, Francis L. Sullivan, Jean Simmons, and Finlay Currie, is released to great acclaim in the UK.
- December 31 – President Harry S. Truman delivers Proclamation 2714, which officially ends hostilities in World War II.

Date unknown

- The 20 mm M61 Vulcan Gatling gun contract is released.
- Female suffrage is enacted in Belgium, Romania, Yugoslavia, Argentina and the Canadian province of Quebec.
- The first female police officers are hired in Korea and Japan.
- The Chinese Civil War intensifies between the Kuomintang and the Communist Party of China.
- The first Tupperware is sold in department and hardware stores.
- The British government takes emergency powers to deal with the balance-of-payments crisis.
- Eva Perón tours Spain, Italy and France on behalf of Argentina, a circuit called the Rainbow Tour.
- The NFL team San Francisco 49ers is formed.
- The Casio company is founded by engineer Tadao Kashio.
- Binghamton University is founded.

Births

January

Diane Keaton

Dolly Parton

- January 1
  - Roberto Rivelino, Brazilian football player
  - Alain Voss, Brazilian-French comics artist (d. 2011)
- January 3
  - John Paul Jones, English rock bassist (Led Zeppelin, Them Crooked Vultures)
  - Cissy King, American dancer and singer
- January 5 – Diane Keaton, American actress and film director

- January 6 – Syd Barrett, English rock guitarist and singer-songwriter (d. 2006)
- January 8
  - Robby Krieger, American rock musician (The Doors)
  - Stanton Peele, American psychologist
- January 9 – Mogens Lykketoft, Danish politician
- January 11
  - Naomi Judd, American country singer
  - John Piper, American theologian
  - Ha Yu, Hong Kong actor
- January 12 – George Duke, American musician (d. 2013)
- January 14
  - Feró Nagy, Hungarian singer
  - Harold Shipman, British serial killer (d. 2004)
- January 16
  - Kabir Bedi, Indian actor
  - Katia Ricciarelli, Italian singer
- January 18 – Joseph Deiss, Swiss Federal Councillor
- January 19
  - Julian Barnes, English novelist
  - Dolly Parton, American singer-songwriter, actress, businesswoman and philanthropist
- January 20 – David Lynch, American film director
- January 21 – Johnny Oates, American baseball player and manager (d. 2004)
- January 22
  - Malcolm McLaren, British music manager (d. 2010)
  - Serge Savard, Canadian hockey player and executive
- January 23 – Arnoldo Alemán, President of Nicaragua
- January 24 – Michael Ontkean, Canadian actor

- January 25 – Géza Bereményi, Hungarian writer, screenwriter and film director
- January 26
    - Gene Siskel, American film critic (d. 1999)
    - Michel Delpech, French singer-songwriter and actor (d. 2016)
- January 27 – Nedra Talley, American singer (The Ronettes)
- January 29 – Bettye LaVette, American soul singer-songwriter
- January 31 – Terry Kath, American rock musician (d. 1978)

February

Alan Rickman

Tyne Daly

- February 1 – Elisabeth Sladen, English actress (d. 2011)

- February 2
  - Isaias Afwerki, President of Eritrea
  - Blake Clark, American actor and comedian
- February 5 – Charlotte Rampling, British actress
- February 6 – Jim Turner, American politician
- February 7 – Pete Postlethwaite, English actor (d. 2011)
- February 9 – Seán Neeson, Northern Irish politician
- February 13 – Colin Matthews, British composer
- February 14
  - Bernard Dowiyogo, President of Nauru (d. 2003)
  - Gregory Hines, American dancer and actor (d. 2003)
- February 19 – Karen Silkwood, American activist (d. 1974)
- February 20 – Brenda Blethyn, English actress
- February 21
  - Tyne Daly, American actress
  - Anthony Daniels, English actor
  - Alan Rickman, English actor (d. 2016)
- February 25
  - Andrew Ang, retired judge of the Supreme Court of Singapore
  - Franz Xaver Kroetz, German dramatist
  - Jean Todt, French motorsport boss
- February 26 – Ahmed H. Zewail, Egyptian chemist, Nobel Prize laureate
- February 28
  - Robin Cook, British politician (d. 2005)
  - Don Francisco, American Christian musician

March

Liza Minnelli

Alejandro Toledo

- March 1
  - Jan Kodeš, Czech tennis player
  - Lana Wood, American actress and producer
- March 4
  - Michael Ashcroft, English entrepreneur
  - Haile Gerima, Ethiopian filmmaker
  - Harvey Goldsmith, British impresario
- March 5
  - Murray Head, English singer and actor
  - Lova Moor, French singer and dancer
- March 6 – David Gilmour, English rock musician (Pink Floyd)

- March 7
  - Okko Kamu, Finnish conductor and violinist
  - Peter Wolf, American rock musician (The J. Geils Band)
- March 10 – Mike Hollands, Australian animator
- March 12
  - Frank Welker, American voice actor and singer
  - Liza Minnelli, American singer and actress
- March 13 – Yonatan Netanyahu, American-born Israeli Army officer, killed in Operation Entebbe (d. 1976)
- March 15 – Bobby Bonds, American baseball player and manager (d. 2003)
- March 17 – Georges J. F. Köhler, German biologist, recipient of the Nobel Prize in Physiology or Medicine (d. 1995)
- March 21 – Timothy Dalton, Welsh actor
- March 25 – Cliff Balsom, English footballer
- March 26 – Johnny Crawford, American child actor and musician
- March 27
  - Olaf Malolepski, German musician (Die Flippers)
  - Mike Jackson, former MLB pitcher.
- March 28 – Alejandro Toledo, former President of Peru
- March 29 – Billy Thorpe, English-born Australian singer-songwriter (d. 2007)
- March 30 – Carolyn Simpson, judge of the Supreme Court of New South Wales
- March 31 – Gonzalo Márquez, Venezuelan Major League Baseball player (d. 1984)

April

János Bródy

Ed O'Neill

Carl XVI Gustaf of Sweden

- April 3 – Hanna Suchocka, Prime Minister of Poland
- April 4 – Dave Hill, English guitarist (Slade)
- April 5
  - Jane Asher, English actress

- o János Bródy, Hungarian singer, guitarist, composer and songwriter
- o Björn Granath, Swedish actor
- April 7
  - o Colette Besson, French track and field athlete (d. 2005)
  - o Léon Krier, Luxembourgian architect
- April 11 – Chris Burden, American artist (d. 2015)
- April 12 – Ed O'Neill, American actor
- April 16 – Margot Adler, American journalist
- April 18 – Hayley Mills, English actress
- April 19 – Tim Curry, British actor, singer and composer
- April 20
  - o Julien Poulin, Canadian actor
  - o Ricardo Maduro, President of Honduras
- April 22 – John Waters, American film director
- April 25
  - o John Fox, British statistician
  - o Talia Shire, American actress
  - o Strobe Talbott, American journalist
  - o Vladimir Zhirinovsky, Russian politician
- April 28 – Larissa Grunig, American public relations theorist and feminist
- April 30 – King Carl XVI Gustaf of Sweden

May

Udo Lindenberg

Cher

- May 1 – Joanna Lumley, English actress and author
- May 2
  - Lesley Gore, American rock singer (d. 2015)
  - Ralf Gothóni, Finnish pianist, conductor and composer
- May 4 – John Watson, Northern Irish racecar driver
- May 5 – Jim Kelly, American actor, martial artist and tennis player (d. 2013)
- May 7
  - Thelma Houston, American singer
  - Michael Rosen, British novelist and poet
- May 9
  - Candice Bergen, American actress
  - Drafi Deutscher, German Schlager singer (d. 2006)

- May 10
  - Graham Gouldman, English songwriter and musician (10cc, Wax)
  - Donovan Leitch, Scottish rock musician
  - Dave Mason, English rock musician (Traffic)
- May 11 – Robert Jarvik, American physicist and artificial heart inventor
- May 12 – Richard Bruce Silverman, John Evans Professor of Chemistry at Northwestern University
- May 15 – Klaus-Peter Siegloch, German journalist
- May 16 – Robert Fripp, British musician
- May 17 – Udo Lindenberg, German musician
- May 18 – Reggie Jackson, American baseball player
- May 19
  - André the Giant, French professional wrestler (d. 1993)
  - Claude Lelièvre, Belgian Commissioner for Children Rights
  - Roger Sloman, English actor
- May 20 – Cher, American actress and rock singer
- May 22
  - George Best, Northern Irish footballer (d. 2005)
  - Howard Kendall, English footballer (d. 2015)
- May 23 – Frederik de Groot, Dutch actor
- May 26 – Mick Ronson, English guitarist (d. 1993)
- May 28 – K. Satchidanandan, Malayalam poet
- May 29 – Fernando Buesa, Basque politician (d. 2000)
- May 30 – Candy Lightner, American founder of Mothers Against Drunk Driving
- May 31 – Adriana Bittel, Romanian writer

June

Donald Trump

Noddy Holder

Ted Shackelford

- June 2
  - Peter Sutcliffe, English serial killer
  - Tomomichi Nishimura, Japanese voice actor

- June 4 – Suzanne Ciani, American pianist and electronic composer
- June 5 – Stefania Sandrelli, Italian actress
- June 7
  - Jenny Jones, Palestinian-Canadian comedian and talk show hostess
  - Robert Tilton, American televangelist and author
- June 8 – Pearlette Louisy, Governor-General of St. Lucia
- June 10 – Fernando Balzaretti, Mexican actor (d. 1998)
- June 13 – Paul L. Modrich, American biochemist, recipient of the Nobel Prize in Chemistry
- June 14 – Donald Trump, American real estate magnate
- June 15
  - Noddy Holder, English rock singer (Slade)
  - Janet Lennon, American singer (The Lennon Sisters)
  - Demis Roussos, Greek singer (d. 2015)
- June 17 – Marcy Kaptur, U.S. Representative for the Ninth Congressional District of Ohio
- June 18
  - Bruce Alexander, English actor
  - Russell Ash, British author (d. 2010)
  - Fabio Capello, Italian football player and manager
- June 20 – Xanana Gusmão, first President of East Timor
- June 22
  - Kay Redfield Jamison, American psychiatrist
  - Józef Oleksy, 7th Prime Minister of Poland (d. 2015)
- June 23 – Ted Shackelford, American actor
- June 24
  - Ellison Onizuka, American astronaut (d. 1986)
  - Robert Reich, 22nd United States Secretary of Labor

- June 26 – Maria von Welser, German TV journalist and President of UNICEF Germany
- June 28 – Gilda Radner, American comedian and actress (d. 1989)
- June 29
    - Egon von Fürstenberg, Swiss fashion designer (d. 2004)
    - Gitte Hænning, Danish singer
    - Ernesto Pérez Balladares, President of Panama

July

George W. Bush

Sylvester Stallone

Cheech Marin

Danny Glover

- July 1
    - Stefan Aust, German journalist and editor-in-chief of the weekly news magazine *Der Spiegel* from 1994 to 2008
    - Mireya Moscoso, President of Panama
- July 2 – Richard Axel, American scientist, recipient of the Nobel Prize in Physiology or Medicine
- July 3 – Leszek Miller, Prime Minister of Poland
- July 4
    - Sam Hunt, New Zealand poet
    - Michael Milken, American financier
    - Ed O'Ross, American actor
- July 6

- George W. Bush, 43rd President of the United States
- Sylvester Stallone, American actor, screenwriter and film director
- July 9
  - Mitch Mitchell, English drummer (The Jimi Hendrix Experience) (d. 2008)
  - Bon Scott, Australian rock singer (AC/DC) (d. 1980)
- July 10 – Sue Lyon, American actress
- July 11 – Jack Wrangler, American porn star (d. 2009)
- July 13 – Cheech Marin, American actor and comedian
- July 14 – John Wood, Australian actor
- July 15 – Linda Ronstadt, American singer and songwriter
- July 16
  - Toshio Furukawa, Japanese voice actor
  - Dave Goelz, American puppeteer
  - Ron Yary, American football player
- July 17 – Alun Armstrong, English actor
- July 19 – Ilie Năstase, Romanian tennis player
- July 22
  - Danny Glover, American actor and film director
  - Mireille Mathieu, French singer
- July 23 – Sally Flynn, American singer
- July 25 – Rita Marley, Jamaican singer
- July 29 – Ximena Armas, Chilean painter
- July 30 – Neil Bonnett, American race car driver (d. 1994)

August

Bill Clinton

- August 1
  - Mike Emrick, American sportscaster
  - Sandi Griffiths, American singer
- August 3 – Jack Straw, English politician
- August 5 – Ron Silliman, American poet
- August 9 – Jim Kiick, American football player
- August 12 – Terry Nutkins, English naturalist (d. 2012)
- August 13 – Janet Yellen, American Chair of the Federal Reserve
- August 16 – Lesley Ann Warren, American actress and singer
- August 17 – Drake Levin, né Levinshefski, American rock guitarist (Paul Revere & the Raiders)
- August 19
  - Charles Bolden, American astronaut
  - Bill Clinton, 42nd President of the United States
  - Beat Raaflaub, Swiss conductor
- August 20
  - Connie Chung, American reporter
  - Ralf Hütter, German techno singer and musician (Kraftwerk)

- N. R. Narayana Murthy, Indian businessman
- August 23 – Keith Moon, English rock drummer (The Who) (d. 1978)
- August 24 – John Grahl, British economist
- August 25
    - Rollie Fingers, American baseball player
    - Charles Ghigna, American poet and children's author
- August 26
    - Valerie Simpson, American singer
    - Mark Snow, American composer
    - Zhou Ji, education minister of the People's Republic of China
- August 29
    - Bob Beamon, American athlete
    - Demetris Christofias, sixth president of Cyprus
    - Leona Gom, Canadian novelist and poet
    -

September

Barry Gibb

Roh Moo-hyun

Billy Preston

Freddie Mercury

Tommy Lee Jones

Oliver Stone

- September 1
  - Barry Gibb, British/Australian rock musician (Bee Gees)
  - Roh Moo-hyun, President of South Korea (d. 2009)
- September 2
  - Luis Ávalos, Cuban-born American character actor
  - Billy Preston, American soul musician (d. 2006)
- September 3 – Francisco Trois, Brazilian chess player
- September 4
  - Gary Duncan, American rock guitarist (Quicksilver Messenger Service)
  - Greg Elmore, American rock drummer (Quicksilver Messenger Service)
- September 5
  - Dennis Dugan, American actor and director

- Freddie Mercury, Zanzibar-born English singer (Queen) (d. 1991)
- September 7
  - Willie Crawford, American baseball player (d. 2004)
  - Francisco Varela, Chilean biologist (d. 2001)
- September 8 – Aziz Sancar, Turkish biochemist, recipient of the Nobel Prize in Chemistry
- September 9
  - Doug Ingle, American rock vocalist (Iron Butterfly)
  - Bruce Palmer, Canadian musician (Buffalo Springfield) (d. 2004)
- September 10
  - Jim Hines, American athlete
  - Don Powell, English rock drummer (Slade)
- September 15
  - Tommy Lee Jones, American actor
  - Oliver Stone, American film director and producer
- September 18 – Akira Kamiya, Japanese voice actor
- September 19 – Connie Kreski, American model (d. 1995)
- September 21
  - Mikhail Kovalchuk, Russian physicist and official
  - Moritz Leuenberger, Swiss Federal Councilor
  - Richard St. Clair, American musician and composer
  - Mart Siimann, Prime Minister of Estonia
- September 23 – Franz Fischler, Austrian politician
- September 24 – Lars Emil Johansen, Prime Minister of Greenland
- September 25
  - Morari Bapu, Hindu Kathakaar
  - Felicity Kendal, British actress

- ○ Jerry Penrod, American bass player
- September 26
  - ○ Andrea Dworkin, American feminist and writer (d. 2005)
  - ○ Radha Krishna Mainali, Nepalese politician
  - ○ Christine Todd Whitman, American politician
- September 28 – Jeffrey Jones, American actor
- September 30
  - ○ Héctor Lavoe, Puerto Rican singer (d. 1993)
  - ○ Claude Vorilhon, French-born 'messenger' of Raëlism
  - ○

October

Susan Sarandon

Sawao Kato

François Bozizé

Craig Venter

- October 1 – Tim O'Brien, American author
- October 2
  - Gen. Sonthi Boonyaratglin, President of the Council for National Security and Commander-in-Chief of the Royal Thai Army
  - Marie-Georges Pascal, French actress
- October 3 – P. P. Arnold, American singer
- October 4 – Susan Sarandon, American actress
- October 6
  - Lloyd Doggett, American politician
  - Renate Holub, German philosopher
- October 7
  - Xue Jinghua, Chinese ballerina

- Catharine MacKinnon, American feminist
- October 8
  - Hanan Ashrawi, Palestinian scholar and legislator
  - John T. Walton, son of Wal-Mart founder Sam Walton (d. 2005)
- October 9 – Tansu Çiller, Turkish politician
- October 10
  - Anne Boyd, Australian musician
  - Mildred Grieveson, British writer
  - Naoto Kan, 61st Prime Minister of Japan
  - Chris Tarrant, British radio and TV personality
- October 11
  - Amitabh Bachchan, Indian actor
  - Daryl Hall, American rock musician (Hall & Oates)
  - Sawao Kato, Japanese gymnast
- October 13
  - Edwina Currie, English politician
  - Dorothy Moore, American singer
  - Demond Wilson, American actor and minister
- October 14
  - Craig Venter, American biotechnologist
  - François Bozizé, President of the Central African Republic
  - Justin Hayward, English rock singer and songwriter (The Moody Blues)
- October 15
  - Richard Carpenter, American pop musician and composer (The Carpenters)
  - John Getz, American actor
  - Marsha Hunt, American singer and novelist

- October 16
  - Suzanne Somers, American actress and singer
  - Elizabeth Witmer, Dutch-born politician
- October 17
  - Vicki Hodge, English actress and model
  - Bob Seagren, American athlete and actor
- October 18
  - James Robert Baker, American novelist, screenwriter
  - Howard Shore, Canadian film composer
  - Andrea Zsadon, Hungarian soprano
- October 19 – Philip Pullman, English author
- October 20
  - Marty Gervais, Canadian writer
  - Elfriede Jelinek, Austrian writer, Nobel Prize laureate
- October 21 – Lyn Allison, Australian politician
- October 22 – Eileen Gordon, British politician
- October 25 – Edith Leyrer, Austrian actress
- October 26 – Pat Sajak, American game-show host
- October 27
  - Leslie L. Byrne, American politician
  - Ivan Reitman, Slovakian-born film director and producer
- October 28 – Sharon Thesen, Canadian poet
- October 29 – Kathryn J. Whitmire, Texas politician; Mayor of Houston, Texas
- October 30
  - Lynne Marta, American actress
  - Andrea Mitchell, American journalist
- October 31 – Stephen Rea, Northern Irish actor

November

Laura Bush

Sally Field

- November 1
  - Ric Grech, British rock bassist (d. 1990)
  - Lynne Russell, American newsreader
- November 2 – Giuseppe Sinopoli, Italian conductor and composer (d. 2001)
- November 4
  - Laura Bush, former First Lady of the United States
  - Les Lannom, American actor and musician
  - Robert Mapplethorpe, American photographer (d. 1989)
- November 5
  - Herman Brood, Dutch artist (d. 2001)

- Loleatta Holloway, American singer (d. 2011)
  - Gram Parsons, American musician (d. 1973)
- November 6 – Sally Field, American actress and singer
- November 7 – Diane Francis, Canadian journalist
- November 8
  - Stella Chiweshe, Zimbabwean musician
  - John Farrar, Australian guitarist, singer and songwriter (The Shadows & Marvin, Welch & Farrar)
  - Guus Hiddink, Dutch football player and manager
- November 10 – Alaina Reed Hall, American actress (d. 2009)
- November 11 – Corrine Brown, American politician
- November 12 – P. P. Arnold, English singer
- November 13 – Ohara Reiko, Japanese actress
- November 14 – Carola Dunn, English writer
- November 15
  - Gwyneth Powell, British actress
  - Sandy Skoglund, American photographer
- November 16
  - Mahasti, Iranian singer (d. 2007)
  - Terence McKenna, writer, philosopher, ethnobotanist and shaman (d. 2000)
- November 17 – Petra Burka, Canadian figure skater
- November 18 – Andrea Allan, Scottish actress
- November 20
  - Greg Cook, American football player (d, 2012)
  - Judy Woodruff, American television reporter
- November 21
  - Emma Cohen, Spanish actress
  - Chaviva Hošek, Czech-born feminist
  - Ulla Jessen, Danish actress

- ○ Jacky Lafon, Belgian actress
- ○ Marina Warner, English writer
- November 22 – Anne Wheeler, Canadian television and film director
- November 23 – Diana Quick, English actress
- November 24 – Ted Bundy, American serial killer (d. 1989)
- November 25 – Marika Lindström, Swedish actress
- November 26 – Ottilia Borbáth, Romanian-Hungarian actress
- November 27
    - ○ Richard Codey, American politician, 53rd Governor of New Jersey
    - ○ Nina Maslova, Russian actress
- November 28 – Regina Braga, Brazilian actress
- November 29
    - ○ Brian Cadd, Australian singer-songwriter
    - ○ Suzy Chaffee, American singer and actress
- November 30
    - ○ Marina Abramović, Yugoslavian performance artist
    - ○ Barbara Cubin, U.S. Congresswoman from Wyoming

December

Gianni Versace

José Carreras

Rhoma Irama

Benny Andersson

Steven Spielberg

- December 2 – Gianni Versace, Italian fashion designer (d. 1997)
- December 3
  - Marjana Lipovšek, Slovenian singer and actress
  - Joop Zoetemelk, Dutch cyclist
- December 4
  - Sherry Alberoni, American actress and voice artist
  - Yō Inoue, Japanese voice actress (d. 2003)
- December 5
  - José Carreras, Spanish tenor
  - Eva-Britt Svensson, Swedish politician
- December 6
  - Nancy Brinker, American health activist and diplomat
  - Chelsea Brown, American actress
- December 8
  - Jacques Bourboulon, French photographer
  - John Rubinstein, American actor
  - Sharmila Tagore, Indian actress
- December 9 – Sonia Gandhi, Indian politician
- December 10
  - Chrystos, American poet

- Thomas Lux, American poet
- December 11
  - Rhoma Irama, Indonesian dangdut musician, actor and politician
  - Susan Kyle, American writer
  - Ellen Meloy, American writer (d. 2004)
- December 12
  - Emerson Fittipaldi, Brazilian racing car driver
  - Gloria Loring, American singer
- December 13 – Nicholas Kollerstrom, British writer
- December 14
  - Jane Birkin, English actress and singer
  - Patty Duke, American actress (d. 2016)
  - Lynne Marie Stewart, American actress
- December 16
  - Benny Andersson, Swedish rock singer and songwriter
  - Alice Aycock, American sculptor
  - Trevor Pinnock, English harpsichordist and conductor
- December 17
  - Eugene Levy, Canadian actor, comedian and director
  - Bel Mooney, English broadcast journalist
- December 18
  - Steve Biko, South African anti-apartheid activist (d. 1977)
  - Nina Škottová, Czech politician and member of the European Parliament
  - Steven Spielberg, American film director
- December 19
  - Candace Pert, American neuroscientist
  - Robert Urich, American actor (d. 2002)

- December 20
  - Lesley Judd, English television presenter
  - John Spencer, American actor (d. 2005)
  - Dick Wolf, American television producer
- December 21
  - Brian Davison, Rhodesian cricketer and Tasmanian politician
  - Carl Wilson, American musician (d. 1998)
- December 23
  - Edita Gruberová, Slovakian soprano
  - Susan Lucci, American actress
  - John Sullivan, English television scriptwriter (d. 2011)
- December 24
  - Jan Akkerman, Dutch rock guitarist (Focus)
  - Roselyne Bachelot-Narquin, French politician and member of the European Parliament
  - Brenda Howard, American bisexual activist (d. 2005)
- December 25
  - Jimmy Buffett, American rock singer and songwriter
  - Larry Csonka, American football player
  - Gene Lamont, American baseball player and manager
- December 27
  - Lenny Kaye, American guitarist
  - Janet Street-Porter, English broadcast journalist
- December 28 – Edgar Winter, American rock musician
- December 29
  - Marianne Faithfull, English singer and actress
  - Ruth Shady, Peruvian archaeologist
- December 30
  - Patti Smith, American poet and singer

- ○ Berti Vogts, German football player and manager
- December 31 – Diane von Fürstenberg, Belgian-American fashion designer

Date unknown

- Tyler Burge, American philosopher
- Jacques Hiron, French journalist and writer
- Ada Mee, German artist
- Kebby Musokotwane, Prime Minister of Zambia (d. 1996)
- Afsaneh Najmabadi, Iranian historian and gender theorist
- Pete Price, Merseyside radio disc jockey
- Rhie Won-bok, South Korean artist

Deaths

January

- January 3 – William Joyce, Irish-American World War II Nazi propaganda broadcaster (known as "Lord Haw-Haw"; b. 1906)
- January 4 – George Woolf, Canadian jockey (b. 1910)
- January 5 – Kitty Cheatham, American singer (b. 1864)
- January 6 – Slim Summerville, American actor (b. 1892)
- January 8 – Dion Fortune, British writer (b. 1890)
- January 9 – Countee Cullen, American poet (b. 1903)
- January 10 – Harry Von Tilzer, American songwriter (b. 1872)
- January 13 – Wilhelm Souchon, German admiral (b. 1864)
- January 15 – Karl Nabersberg, German youth leader (b. 1908)
- January 29 – Harry Hopkins, American politician (b. 1890)

February

Felix Hoffmann

- February 2 – Rondo Hatton, American actor (b. 1894)
- February 5 – George Arliss, English actor (b. 1868)

- February 6 – Oswald Kabasta, Austrian conductor (suicide) (b. 1896)
- February 8
    - Felix Hoffmann, German chemist (b. 1868)
    - Miles Mander, English actor (b. 1888)
- February 15 – Cornelius Johnson, American athlete (b. 1913)
- February 17 – Dorothy Gibson, American actress (b. 1889)
- February 19 – Rafael Erich, Prime Minister of Finland (b. 1879)
- February 21 – Theodore Stark Wilkinson, American admiral (b. 1888)
- February 23 – Tomoyuki Yamashita, Japanese general (b. 1885)
- February 25 – René Le Grèves, French cyclist (b. 1910)

March

- March 2 – George E. Stewart, American Medal of Honor recipient (b. 1872)
- March 4 – Bror von Blixen-Finecke, Danish big-game hunter (b. 1886)
- March 14 – Werner von Blomberg, German field marshal (b. 1878)
- March 23 – Gilbert N. Lewis, American chemist (b. 1875)
- March 24
    - Alexander Alekhine, Russian chess player (b. 1892)
    - Carl Schuhmann, German athlete (b. 1869)
- March 31 – John Vereker, 6th Viscount Gort, British Field Marshal (b. 1886)

April

- April 1
    - Noah Beery, Sr., American actor (b. 1882)
    - Edward Sheldon, American playwright (b. 1886)
- April 2 – Kate Bruce, veteran silent screen actress, made many films with D. W. Griffith (b. 1858)
- April 3
    - Alf Common, English footballer (b. 1880)
    - Masaharu Homma, Japanese general (executed) (b. 1887)
- April 5 – Vincent Youmans, American composer (b. 1898)
- April 8 – Qin Bangxian, General Secretary of the Communist Party of China (b. 1907)
- April 14 – Otto Dowling, United States Navy Captain and the 25th Governor of American Samoa (b. 1881)
- April 20 – Mae Busch, American actress (b. 1891)
- April 21 – John Maynard Keynes, British economist (b. 1883)
- April 22
    - Lionel Atwill, English actor (b. 1885)
    - Harlan F. Stone, Chief Justice of the United States (b. 1872)

May

- May 1 – Bill Johnston, American tennis champion (b. 1894)
- May 16
    - Bruno Tesch, German chemist and Nazi war criminal (executed) (b. 1890)

- o Karl Weinbacher, German manager and war criminal (executed) (b. 1898)
- May 19 – Booth Tarkington, American novelist (b. 1869)
- May 20 – Jacob Ellehammer, Danish inventor (b. 1871)
- May 31 – Picoğlu Osman, Turkish kemenche player (b. 1901)

June

Ion Antonescu

Gerhart Hauptmann

- June 1
  - o Ion Antonescu, Romanian prime minister and dictator (executed) (b. 1882)
  - o Leo Slezak, German tenor (b. 1873)
- June 3 – Chen Gongbo, 2nd President of Republic of China during Nanjing regime (executed) (b. 1892)

- June 5 – Maud Watson, English tennis player, first female Wimbledon champion (b. 1864)
- June 6 – Gerhart Hauptmann, German writer, Nobel Prize laureate (b. 1862)
- June 9 – Ananda Mahidol, King of Siam (b. 1925)
- June 10 – Jack Johnson, African-American boxer (b. 1878)
- June 13 – Charles Butterworth, American actor (b. 1896)
- June 14
  - John Logie Baird, Scottish television pioneer (b. 1888)
  - Edward Bowes, American radio personality (b. 1874)
- June 19 – Theodor Wulf, German physicist and Jesuit (b. 1868)
- June 20 – Empress Wanrong China (b. 1906)
- June 23 – William S. Hart, stage actor and silent film cowboy star (b. 1864/1865)
- June 27 – Wanda Gág, American artist, author, translator and illustrator (b. 1893)
- June 28 – Antoinette Perry, American actress and director (b. 1888)

July

- July – Howard Hyde Russell, American temperance advocate, founder of the Anti-Saloon League (b. 1855)
- July 2 – Mary Alden, American stage and screen actress (b. 1883)
- July 4
  - Jenny-Wanda Barkmann, German Nazi overseer at Stutthof concentration camp (executed) (b. ca. 1922)

- Elisabeth Becker, German Nazi overseer at Stutthof concentration camp (executed) (b. 1923)
- Wanda Klaff, German Nazi overseer at Stutthof concentration camp (executed) (b. 1922)
- Ewa Paradies, German Nazi overseer at Stutthof concentration camp (executed) (b. 1920)
- Gerda Steinhoff, German Nazi overseer at Stutthof concentration camp (executed) (b. 1922)
- July 8 – Orrick Glenday Johns, American writer (b. 1887)
- July 12 – Ray Stannard Baker, American journalist and author (b. 1870)
- July 13 – Alfred Stieglitz, American photographer (b. 1864)
- July 15 – Razor Smith, English cricketer (b. 1877)
- July 17 – Campbell Tait, Governor of Southern Rhodesia (b. 1886)
- July 20 – Shiro Kawase, Japanese admiral (b. 1889)
- July 27 – Gertrude Stein, American writer (b. 1874)

August

H. G. Wells

- August 5 – Wilhelm Marx, Chancellor of Germany (b. 1863)
- August 6

- Blanche Bingley Hillyard, English tennis champion (b. 1863)
- Tony Lazzeri, American baseball player (New York Yankees) and MLB Hall of Famer (b. 1903)
- August 9 – Léon Gaumont, French film pioneer (b. 1864)
- August 12 – Inayatullah Khan, former King of Afghanistan (b. 1888)
- August 13 – H. G. Wells, English science fiction writer and historian (b. 1866)
- August 20 – "Rags" Ragland, American comedian and actor (b. 1905)
- August 26 – Jeanie MacPherson, American actress (b. 1887)
- August 28 – Florence Turner, American actress (b. 1885)
- August 29 – John Steuart Curry, American painter (b. 1897)

September

- September 16
  - Henri Gouraud, French general (b. 1867)
  - James Hopwood Jeans, English physicist, astronomer and mathematician (b. 1877)
- September 17 – Frank Burke, American baseball player (b. 1880)
- September 25 – Heinrich George, German actor (b. 1893)
- September 29 – Raimu, French actor (b. 1883)
- September 30 – Takashi Sakai, Japanese general (b. 1887)

October

- October 2 – Ignacy Mościcki, former President of Poland (b. 1867)

- October 4 – Barney Oldfield, American race car driver and automobile pioneer (b. 1878)
- October 6 – Per Albin Hansson, Prime Minister of Sweden (b. 1885)
- October 12 – Joseph Stilwell, American World War II general (b. 1883)
- October 15 – Hermann Göring, German Nazi Reichsmarschall (suicide) (b. 1893)
- October 16
  - Hans Frank, German Nazi Governor General of Poland (executed) (b. 1900)
  - Wilhelm Frick, German Nazi Minister of the Interior (executed) (b. 1877)
  - Alfred Jodl, German general and World War II Chief of the German armed forces (executed) (b. 1890)
  - Ernst Kaltenbrunner, German Nazi police general (executed) (b. 1903)
  - Wilhelm Keitel, German field marshal (executed) (b. 1882)
  - Joachim von Ribbentrop, German Nazi foreign minister (executed) (b. 1893)
  - Alfred Rosenberg, German Nazi ideologist (executed) (b. 1893)
  - Fritz Sauckel, German Nazi general plenipotentiary (executed) (b. 1892)
  - Arthur Seyss-Inquart, Austrian Nazi leader (executed) (b. 1892)
  - Julius Streicher, German Nazi propaganda publisher (executed) (b. 1885)

November

- November 5 – Joseph Stella, Italian-American painter (b. 1877)
- November 7 – Henry Lehrman, American actor (b. 1886)
- November 11 – Nikolay Burdenko, Russian surgeon, founder of Russian neurosurgery (b. 1876)
- November 14 – Manuel de Falla, Spanish composer (b. 1876)
- November 18 – Donald Meek, Scottish actor (b. 1878)
- November 24 – László Moholy-Nagy, Hungarian painter and photographer (b. 1895)
- November 25 – George Gandy, American entrepreneur (b. 1851)

December

- December 5 – Louis Dewis, Belgian Post-Impressionist painter (b. 1872)
- December 7
  - Laurette Taylor, American actress (b. 1884)
  - Sada Yacco, Japanese stage actress (b. 1871)
- December 10
  - Walter Johnson, American baseball player (Washington Senators) and MLB Hall of Famer (b. 1887)
  - Damon Runyon, American writer (b. 1880)
- December 12 – Renée Falconetti, French actress (b. 1892)
- December 13 – Curtis Hidden Page, New Hampshire politician (b. 1870)
- December 14 – Tom Dowse, Irish major league baseball player in the 1890s (b. 1866)

- December 23 – John A. Sampson, American gynecologist (b. 1873)
- December 25
  - W. C. Fields, American actor and comedian (b. 1880)
  - Henri Le Fauconnier, French painter (b. 1881)
- December 28 – Carrie Jacobs-Bond, American singer and songwriter (b. 1862)

Nobel Prizes

- Physics – Percy Williams Bridgman
- Chemistry – James B. Sumner, John Howard Northrop, Wendell Meredith Stanley
- Physiology or Medicine – Hermann Joseph Muller
- Literature – Hermann Hesse
- Peace – Emily Greene Balch, John Mott

In the News.

Jan 22nd US president sets up CIA, Central Intelligence Agency.

Feb 10th Charles "Lucky" Luciano is deported to Italy, and never returns to the United States.

Mar 22nd 1st US rocket to leave the Earth's atmosphere (50 miles up)

Apr 1st Weight Watchers forms.

May 2nd The "Battle of Alcatraz" takes place, killing two guards and three inmates.

Jun 3rd 1st bikini bathing suit displayed (Paris)

Oct 1st 12 Nazi war criminals sentenced to death in Nuremberg.

Sep 18th Joe Louis KOs Tami Mauriello in 1 for heavyweight boxing title.

Dec 21st Earthquake in South Japan, kills 1,086.

1946 Calendar

January 1946
Sun	Mon	Tue	Wed	Thu	Fri	Sat
		1	2	3	4	5
6	7	8	9	10	11	12
13	14	15	16	17	18	19
20	21	22	23	24	25	26
27	28	29	30	31		

February 1946
Sun	Mon	Tue	Wed	Thu	Fri	Sat
					1	2
3	4	5	6	7	8	9
10	11	12	13	14	15	16
17	18	19	20	21	22	23
24	25	26	27	28		

March 1946
Sun	Mon	Tue	Wed	Thu	Fri	Sat
					1	2
3	4	5	6	7	8	9
10	11	12	13	14	15	16
17	18	19	20	21	22	23
24	25	26	27	28	29	30
31						

April 1946
Sun	Mon	Tue	Wed	Thu	Fri	Sat
	1	2	3	4	5	6
7	8	9	10	11	12	13
14	15	16	17	18	19	20
21	22	23	24	25	26	27
28	29	30				

May 1946
Sun	Mon	Tue	Wed	Thu	Fri	Sat
			1	2	3	4
5	6	7	8	9	10	11
12	13	14	15	16	17	18
19	20	21	22	23	24	25
26	27	28	29	30	31	

June 1946
Sun	Mon	Tue	Wed	Thu	Fri	Sat
						1
2	3	4	5	6	7	8
9	10	11	12	13	14	15
16	17	18	19	20	21	22
23	24	25	26	27	28	29
30						

July 1946
Sun	Mon	Tue	Wed	Thu	Fri	Sat
	1	2	3	4	5	6
7	8	9	10	11	12	13
14	15	16	17	18	19	20
21	22	23	24	25	26	27
28	29	30	31			

August 1946
Sun	Mon	Tue	Wed	Thu	Fri	Sat
				1	2	3
4	5	6	7	8	9	10
11	12	13	14	15	16	17
18	19	20	21	22	23	24
25	26	27	28	29	30	31

September 1946
Sun	Mon	Tue	Wed	Thu	Fri	Sat
1	2	3	4	5	6	7
8	9	10	11	12	13	14
15	16	17	18	19	20	21
22	23	24	25	26	27	28
29	30					

October 1946
Sun	Mon	Tue	Wed	Thu	Fri	Sat
		1	2	3	4	5
6	7	8	9	10	11	12
13	14	15	16	17	18	19
20	21	22	23	24	25	26
27	28	29	30	31		

November 1946
Sun	Mon	Tue	Wed	Thu	Fri	Sat
					1	2
3	4	5	6	7	8	9
10	11	12	13	14	15	16
17	18	19	20	21	22	23
24	25	26	27	28	29	30

December 1946
Sun	Mon	Tue	Wed	Thu	Fri	Sat
1	2	3	4	5	6	7
8	9	10	11	12	13	14
15	16	17	18	19	20	21
22	23	24	25	26	27	28
29	30	31